Knot Tying M

C000171620

The Ultimate Guide on How to Identify, Tie and Untie All Manner of Everyday Knots in Different Styles for Campers, Rock Climbers, Sailors, Shoes, Animals, & Other Everyday Uses Or Activities

Introduction

Ropes are essential survival tools that you can use in different circumstances. However, without knowing how to tie and use different knots for different, unique situations, the rope will not be of any help to you. It only becomes useful when you acquire the necessary knowledge.

This book will equip you with the essential knot tying skills you need to know.

Table of Content

Chapter 1: Knot Tying 101

As you learn how to work with different kinds of knots, you will encounter a lot of new words.

Without understanding what these words and phrases mean, the knot tying instructions in this book can be quite confusing.

In this chapter, we shall look at and explain the most commonly used knot tying terminologies, categories of knots, and introduce you to knot tying principles you should keep in mind:

First, let's look at an illustration of the primary sections of a knot tying model and rope.

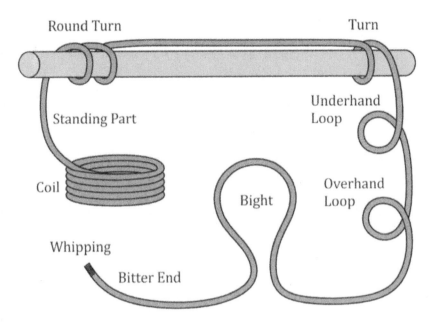

Now that the image above has given you an idea of the various parts involved in knot tying, let's discuss what each is:

Knot Tying Terminologies

The most common knot tying terminologies are:

#: Working end/whipping

Also called the running end or tag end, the working end is the free end of the rope you are working with when tying a knot.

#: Standing end & standing part

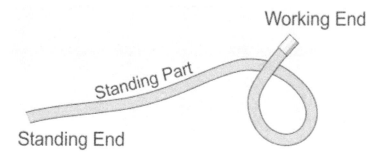

The Standing end is the end of the rope that you don't manipulate when tying a knot. On the other hand, the standing part is the length of rope that faces the standing end; you also don't manipulate this part.

#: Bight

The bight is a sharp curve with a small radius in a rope. It's where the standing and working parts come in contact or near one another. This term can also mean any part of the rope excluding the ends.

For instance, a knot 'tied on the bight' is one where you tie the rope around the middle without manipulating any of the ends.

#: Bitter end

The bitter end is the last 1-2 inches of a rope and is often a short section with which to work.

#: Loop

The loop is similar to a bight. The main difference between the two is that the curve has a larger radius, and the loop covers more area. This term may also refer to the part of the loop's knot or any other rope structure that encircles an object completely.

#: Crossing point/turn

The turn is a curve where the rope crosses over itself once. For instance, if you twist a bight to 180 degrees, you end up with a crossing turn.

#: Elbow

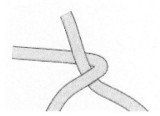

If you take the bight and twist it to an angle of 360 degrees, the elbow will be the section formed between the standing part & working end at the bottom and the crossing turn at the top.

#: Underhand and overhand

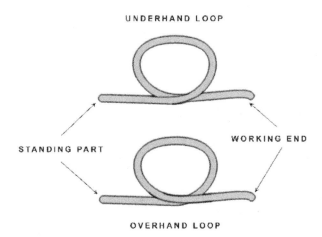

The overhand is a crossing turn where the working end loops over the standing part, while the underhand is a crossing turn where the standing part loops on top of the working part.

#: Turn

A turn is half a revolution of a rope around an object, such that both ends are facing the same direction, without encircling the object completely.

#: Round turn

A round turn is a full revolution of a rope around a given object. The rope may wind 360 degrees around an object such that both ends face opposite directions.

The rope may also wind 540 degrees around a given object, such that both ends face the same direction. If the rope encircles the object in a couple of adjacent round turns, we call each of the revolutions a wrap.

#: Hank

Hank is a word used to describe lengths of rope.

Learning about knots demands that you know about the various categories of knots:

Categories Of Knots

Here are the most common categories of knots:

#: Loops

These are knots used to hold or create attachment points in a rope.

To tie it, you should tie the rope to itself to form a closed loop that you can then put around an object like a tree. These types of knot types may fit tightly or loosely around the object, and in most cases, the size is adjustable fit the object.

#: Hitches

These are knots made to tie a rope onto an object at one end. As opposed to loop knots, hitches highly depend on an object for their structure; thus, they cannot exist independently.

#: Bends

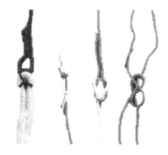

Bends are knots used to tie two different ropes together, including ropes of varying diameters

#: Lashings

These are knots used to hold two objects together. They generally work by wrapping or turning numerous rounds around two objects. These knots mostly apply to the process of building structures.

To get started with knot tying, you also need to internalize a few fundamental principles:

Knot Tying General Principles

A couple of general principles govern how we tie knots to ensure that they work efficiently.

Fundamentally, the most important thing you need to keep in mind is that when it comes to tying a perfect knot, the basic rule of thumb is to ensure that *it is easy to tie and untie and that it serves a specific purpose.*

Other principles include:

- The knot must be firm and tied tight enough such that slipping is impossible.

- The knot must be as small as possible to reduce excessive amounts of reactions when the knot comes into contact with absorbable substances.

- When tying a knot, ensure that it leaves room for no friction (sawing) in between the strands as this might weaken its integrity.

- When handling the rope, be very careful to avoid damaging it or causing weaknesses

Let's now discuss the various types of knots and their possible applications:

Chapter 2: Basic Knots

This chapter will introduce you to basic knots, show you how to tie them, and outline the advantages and disadvantages of each:

Basic Knots

Basic knots include

#: Overhand Knot

The overhand knot is one of the most common and most basic knots that most people know how to tie. It is the foundation for countless other knots and can also work as a stopper knot.

How to tie it

- Start by forming an overhand loop

- Thread the working end upward from underneath the loop

- Pull both the standing part and the working end to tighten the knot

This knot works best when applied at the end of a rope, which helps prevent it from becoming untied at the application of tension.

Advantages

Tying it is straightforward

Disadvantages

Depending on the type of rope used to tie this knot, if put under heavy loads, it can be very hard to untie, especially true if tied using very thin cordage.

Possible applications

You can use this knot can be applied when hanging a tarp. You can tie an overhand knot at the end of the rope to prevent it from sliding through the tarp's grommet.

#: The Figure 8 Knot

The figure 8 knot is another knot that you can use as a stopper knot; it's the building block for most common knots.

How to tie

- Start by forming an overhand loop

- Move the working end the standing part then around it

- Thread your working end down through the resulting loop

- Pull to tighten the knot. The result will be a knot that resembles the number 8, as illustrated above

Advantages

The figure 8 knot is very easy to tie and also easy to untie compared to the overhand knot. It is also bulkier than the overhand knot, which makes it stronger.

Disadvantages

Depending on the type of rope used to tie this knot, if it is put under heavy loads, it can be hard to untie.

Possible applications

- Since the figure-eight knot can work as a stopper knot, it can come in handy in situations where the overhand knot might slip through the hole because it is larger than the overhand knot, which makes it harder for it to slip through.

- This knot works best as a base formation for most of the complex knots used by rock climbers.

]#: Square Knot

The square knot is one of the most popular knots, mostly used to bind objects together. Some areas of the globe call it the reef knot.

Although this knot is very popular, you should use it with a lot of caution. Most people tend to use it to join two lengths of rope to create a longer rope, which is not safe because square knots tend to slip or even become untied when a load is applied.

How to tie

Hold the ends of your rope in each hand. As you do this, cross the working end in your left hand over to the one in your right hand, which will result in an 'X.'

Wrap the working end you are holding in your left hand behind then under the working end that you are holding in your right hand.

Continue wrapping the working end until it lies over the working end in your left hand—shown below

Proceed by taking the working end in your right hand then cross it over to the working end on your left hand to form another 'X.'

Wrap the working of the rope in your right hand behind then under the working end in your left hand

Continue to wrap until the working end lies over the working end in your left hand—shown below

Now you have a standing part and working end in each of your hands. Pull them away from each other to tighten the knot.

NOTE: If you tie this knot incorrectly, you will end up with a 'granny knot.' To know whether you have tied your knot correctly, check the sides.

A proper knot should have a standing part and working end over a bight. If this is not the case, then you probably tied a granny knot. Below is an instance of a square knot tied improperly.

Advantages

This knot is simple to tie and untie

Disadvantages

As mentioned earlier, this knot is not suitable for some situations, especially those that involve heavy loads. If used in such situations, it can result in injuries or even death.

When this knot is not under any tension, it can easily become untied or shake loose.

Possible applications

- You can use this knot to secure a bandage to limbs such as legs or arms.

- If you are camping and have gone out to collect some twigs for a fire, you can use this type of knot to bind your bundle together so that it's easier to carry.

- In a case where you need a makeshift belt, you can tie a length of rope around your waist and fasten it using a square knot.

#: Bowline Knot

The bowline knot is effective in cases where you might need to tie a loop at your rope's end or when you need to secure your rope around an object.

How to tie

Start by forming an overhand loop on the rope's standing part.

Move the working end of the rope upward through the resulting loop from step 1

Wrap the working end of the rope behind its standing part

Continue to move the working end into and through the overhand loop you created in step 1

Complete the knot and pull it until it is tight enough

Advantages

This knot is easy to tie and untie; it's also fairly secure. When you add load onto a rope with this knot, it tends to tighten up, not become untied, which is usually the case with most other knots.

This knot will also not constrict to the object to which you've tied it around upon application of tension to the rope's standing part.

Disadvantages

Any tension exerted on a rope with this knot makes the knot almost impossible to untie—or untying it becomes very challenging.

Possible applications

This knot has a wide range of applications. For instance, you can use it to secure the guy line of a tent. You can also use it to secure and tether a canoe or raft to a tree as it floats in water.

Chapter 3: Knots For Campers

Below are camper-friendly knots

#: Midshipman's Hitch

Almost similar to a knot called the taut-line hitch, the midshipman's hitch is a more secure option.

This knot is effective for situations where you are securing an object to an anchor point using a length of rope, and you need to adjust the tension. Once tied, this knot allows you to slide it easily along the main rope to either decrease or increase tension.

When you apply a load to the standing part of the rope, the knot stays in that position. It does not slip based on the friction generated between the rope and the knot.

How to tie

Start by passing the working end around the desired object to make a turn—shown in the image below:

Now cross your working end over the standing part of the rope

Wrap your working end around and under the ropes standing part, ensuring that the wrap is inside the loop.

Continue wrapping the working end around the first turn, ensuring that you cross over the turn and keep the second turn in the loop's part that is closest to you—shown below.

The second turn should form a crossing point over the first turn, which is responsible for creating extra friction, hence making the knot more secure.

Apply some tension to your working end to stop the knot from slipping as you complete this knot.

Continue to wrap using your working end, but this time, on the outer part of the loop. Pass your working end behind the rope's standing part—shown below

Thread your working end into the hole in the wrap you created. By doing this, you will be making a half hitch on the outer part of the loop that you formed on the standing part.

30

Dress the knot and pull to tighten it before applying a load. Your knot is now complete and should look like the one in the image below.

How to adjust

You can adjust this knot by grabbing it in your hand and sliding it either upwards on its standing part to make the loop bigger, or downwards to make the loop smaller.

Advantages

It is easy and quick to make adjustments to guylines with a midshipman's hitch tied onto them. Unlike other knots of similar applications, you can tie this knot when there is a load already tied on the standing part of the rope.

Disadvantages

This knot is not an ideal choice for situations where there'll be considerable amounts of tension applied to the rope. That's because the knot primarily relies on friction to prevent it from sliding, and more tension may require high amounts of friction to keep it in place. The friction generated may be insufficient to hold the tension from the load; thus, the knot will end up sliding.

The choice of material for the rope is also an important factor to consider here because slippery-type of ropes will not be able to hold their position because of a lack of sufficient friction.

Possible applications

You can use this knot to attach guylines to a tent stake, which works because after you tie the knot, you can apply tension to the guyline by sliding the knot up the standing part.

You can also use it when you want to take the tent down by sliding the knot towards the part to which you have anchored it to release the tension exerted on the guyline.

You can also use this knot to secure a rope to a tree when putting up a tarp shelter's rigid line.

You can also use it to create a makeshift clothesline.

#: Sheet Bend Knot

Also called a weavers knot, this knot is mostly ideal in cases where you have to join two ropes that have different diameters. However, it's not limited to ropes that have varying diameters; you can also use it to join ropes with similar diameters.

How to tie

Start by making a bight on the working end of the rope with the thicker diameter. Hold it in your right hand.

Keep the 'U' of the bight facing the right and the ropes working at the bight's top.

Then take the rope with the thinner diameter and thread it upwards from the bottom of the bight you formed in step 1

Now move the working of the thin rope around and behind the bight of the other rope. It is essential to wrap it in such a way that it goes towards the direction the working end of the thick rope is facing

Thread the working end of the rope with the smaller diameter under itself—shown in the image below

Dress and then finally tighten your knot

NOTE: If you do not follow the above steps correctly, you might end up with the working ends of the two ropes on the

opposite side of your knot, which will make your knot very likely to slip because of tension.

To make sure you've tied the knot correctly, make sure both working ends of the ropes are facing the top of the knot.

Advantages

Even though tying knots using ropes of different diameters can cause the knot to become unstable and prone to slipping, this knot can solve this issue.

Disadvantages

This knot tends to get loose when you apply tension on both ropes

Possible applications

If you need a longer rope, and all you have is the option of using different types of scavenged rope, all of which have different diameters, then this knot will come in handy.

#: Double Sheet Bend

The double sheet bend is a slight modification to the sheet bend knot but purposed to become more secure.

How to tie

Form a bight using the working end of the rope with the thick diameter and hold it in your left hand.

Keep the 'U' of the bight facing the right; you should position the working end at the top of the bight.

Hold the thinner rope in your right hand and thread it from the bottom of the bight going upwards.

Move the working end of the thin rope around and behind the bight. Wrap it towards the direction that the bight's working end is facing (shown in the above steps).

Thread the working end of the thin rope under itself, then create a second wrap by repeating steps 4 and 5.

Finish by tightening and dressing the knot. You will end up with a knot that looks like the one in the image below:

Possible applications

You can use this knot anywhere where you would need to use a sheet bend knot and in situations where you need a more secure knot

#: The Double Fisherman's Knot

In some situations, you may need to tie together two lengths of rope to make a longer one. This knot, in some cases referred to as the 'grapevine knot,' is what you should use in such circumstances.

This knot is a constituent of two knots that lock onto each other when you apply tension to the rope.

How to tie

Start by Laying the working ends of each of the ropes parallel to one another. Let the ends overlap by a few inches—shown in the image below. The diameter of the rope you are using will determine how much overlap you need to have. Thin ropes such as paracord will require a little overlap compared to thicker ropes that may need more overlap. As you continue to practice with this knot, you will be able to develop a sense of how much overlap you should leave.

Cross the working end of your rope over to the other ropes standing part and wrap behind it. Then move around it to the top—shown in the image below.

Form another wrap, ensuring you keep it on the left side of the crossing point of the previous wrap—shown below.

Thread your working end through the two wraps you formed—moving the rope below the crossing points on the two wraps.

Dress the knot and pull to tighten it. At this stage, you have completed the first part of the knot. The next part involves repeating the whole process on the other length of rope.

Cross the working end of the rope over to the other rope's standing part. When you complete this step, you should end up with the working end facing downwards—shown in the image below.

Create another wrap, ensuring you keep it at the right side of the crossing point you formed in step 6.

Thread the working end under the crossing points of both the wraps you created. Dress the knot and pull to tighten it. You have now completed the second part of the knot—which should be looking like the image below.

To complete the knot, pull on each of the standing parts of the two ropes. The knots will slide together, and you will end up with a knot like the one shown below.

NOTE: If you tied the knot properly, you should have a tidy and neat appearance where the two knots lie neatly against each other. When you look at the knots from the side, each of them should look like an 'X.' When you flip it, the knots should look like four diagonal lines running in parallel. The working ends from the two ropes should end up on opposite sides of the diagonals. If they are on the same side, then you have probably made a mistake, which means you will need to repeat the steps afresh.

Variation Of The Double Fisher Man's Knot

You can form an extra wrap before threading the working end under the crossing points on each knot. In this case, you will end up with the triple fisherman's knot.'

Advantages

Based on the design of this knot, it is the most effective way to tie up two lengths of rope—as it is more secure compared to other knots—to join multiple lengths of rope.

Disadvantages

When you place a heavy load on a rope with this type of knot, it can become challenging to unite it. In some cases, this knot can also be very tricky to tie.

Possible applications

In situations where you have to work with scavenged
cordage, you can use this type of knot to tie together topes of
multiple lengths to create one long and strong length of rope.

Chapter 4: Knots For Sailors & Fishermen

The most common sailing and fishing knots are:

#: Blood Knot

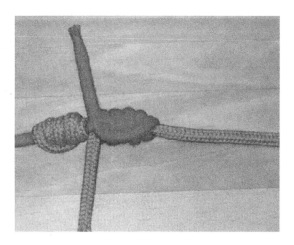

This knot is the one fishermen often use to join lines of different sizes.

How to tie

Hold the working end of the rope with the thicker diameter in your left hand and the other rope in your right hand. Cross the two lines over each other to form an 'X.' The thicker line should lie behind the thinner line.

With the index finger and thumb of your right hand, pinch the crossing point of the two lines and hold it firmly.

Wrap the working end of the thinner line around the rope with the thicker diameter in a counterclockwise direction. That means you should pass the thinner rope behind the thick one, then over the top, and finally towards you— complete at least 4-5 wraps. Once you complete the final wrap, it should be pointing downwards.

Next, pull the working end of the thinner rope towards the crossing point you made earlier, making sure that the working end of the thinner rope points upwards and lies on top of its standing part—shown in the image below.

Next, pinch the knot at the location where they meet, using your left hand to hold it in place as you continue.

Now wrap the working end of the thinner rope in a clockwise manner. That means you will have to pass the thicker line in front of the thinner rope, under it, and then finally towards you.

Make the same number of wraps you did in step 3 to make the knot symmetrical. When done, the working end should point upwards—shown below.

Now pass the working end of the thicker rope towards the working end of the thinner line. Note that the working end of the thinner rope will have to tread through the hole between the two lines pointing upwards. You should also thread the working end of the thicker rope through the same hole, though for this one, you should pass it from the top so that it points downwards.

If you correctly do this, then the working end of the thinner rope should point upwards while the working end of the thicker rope should point downwards—shown below.

The next step is to dress the knot as lightly as possible and lubricate it.

Pull the standing part of the two ropes to bring everything into place.

Once you have everything set, quickly pull the standing part again to tighten the knot. It may take a few attempts before you get it right. The appearance of the knot will change completely

Trim off the excess rope on the working ends as close to the knot as possible. The finished knot should look like the one below.

Knot Tying Made Easy

Advantages

When tied properly, this knot is very sleek and can pass through the rod guides of a fishing pole easily. The streamlined nature of this knot also helps keep it from collecting debris like water moss.

Disadvantages

This knot is not easy to learn or tie.

Note: For this knot, the blue rope represents the thicker line, while the red one represents the thinner line.

Possible applications

You can use this knot to make to create tapered leaders, which allows your fly-fishing line to roll out smoothly and settle on the water gently without making a splash.

#: Surgeon's Knot

The surgeon's knot is another useful fishing knot, mainly used to join two lengths of line. However, unlike the blood knot, this one only works with two lines that have an almost exact or similar diameter. Drastically differing diameters will not work with this knot.

How to tie

Start by laying the main fishing line and the new section you are tying in parallel to each other. Have the working end of both ropes overlap each other by a few inches. The two lines should also be pointing in the same direction.

Form the overlapped sections of both ropes into an overhand loop.

Pass the working ends of the two lines through the loop you created to form a simple overhand knot.

Now repeat the previous step so that you can have a knot that appears like the one shown below.

Lubricate it and then pull to tighten it. To complete the knot, just trim off the working ends as close as possible to the knot

Advantages

This knot is very strong and extremely simple to tie. It also does not weaken the line—as is the case with other knots

Disadvantages

This knot is not suitable for tying a long extension onto your reel because you cannot easily tie it in the middle of the line.

The knot is also larger in diameter than the blood knot; thus, it might cause jams in some fishing rods.

NOTE: The red rope represents the longer fishing line connected to your reel. The blue rope represents the shorter section of the tippet or leader supposed to tie onto the end of your mainline.

Possible applications

You can use this knot to tie a leader onto your fishing line or to tie tippets at the end of fly-fishing leaders.

#: Palomar Knot

Being one of the knots used most used by fishermen, here's how to tie the Palomar knot:

How to tie

Start by threading the working end of your line into the eyelet of your lure or hook.

Then pass your working end back through the hook's eyelet —as shown below. You will end up with a bight going through the eyelet.

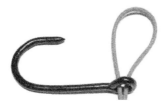

Next, cross your bight over both the standing part and working end of your line—shown below.

Now tie a loose overhand knot using the bight as you take care not to twist it. However, do not tighten the knot all the way at this level. Leave it a bit loose.

Pass the bight over the lure or hook—shown below.

Next, move your bight gently towards the standing end of your line. Ensure you pass your bight over and around the overhand you created in step 4.

Then pull the standing part and the working end slowly to allow the knot to tighten. Before the knot tightens all the way, lubricate it.

Hold the lure or hook carefully as you pull the standing part and the working end to fully tighten the knot.

Snip off the working end as close to the knot as possible. Your Palomar knot is now complete.

Advantages

This knot is compatible with most fishing lines and does not slip as much as other knots.

Most of the fishing lines available in the market today have different features that affect their ability to hold knots without slipping. The Palomar knot is ideal as it can hold a knot without slipping, whether you are using the latest fishing lines or typical monofilament fishing lines.

Disadvantages

If tied incorrectly, then it might not work well with some types of fishing lines, thus causing your line to have higher chances of breaking at the knot.

Possible applications

This knot's main use is to tie a lure or hook onto a fishing line

#: The Figure 8 Loop

If you want a knot that is more secure than the figure 8 knot, you can consider going for the figure 8 loop, which is commonly used by rock climbers and mountaineers.

How to tie

Start by forming a bight in the position where you want to tie your figure 8 loop.

Next, form an underhand loop on the bight.

Now move the bight's head over the standing part and the working end then around the two.

Continue to move it through the loop, and then dress the resulting knot by flipping the part near the loop. Pull it hard to tighten it

Advantages

The figure 8 loop knot is easy to tie at any position, even the middle of the rope, as long as there is no tension applied.

Disadvantages

Depending on the type of rope used, you might struggle to untie this knot if there is a considerable amount of tension applied to the rope.

Possible applications

You can use this knot by attaching an object to it's working end or to a section of the rope's standing part. You can also create a loop on the standing part, which you can then use to tie another rope onto, which can come in handy in various situations such as securing loads to a boat or a trailer.

#: Two Half Hitch

Also called the double half hitch, you can tie this knot is simply by tying two half hitch knots. A half hitch knot is an overhand hand knot tied onto an object. It is a kind of binding knot used to attach cordage onto objects like trees. Tying two ½ hitch knots makes it more secure.

How to tie

Hold the working end of the rope in your hand and pass it around an object of your choice, which will form a single turn.

Next, pass the working end to the front of the rope's standing part—shown in the image below.

Thread the working of the rope through the loop you created in the previous step and pull to tighten, which will be your first half hitch.

Now pass the working end of the rope around its standing part again. However, this time, keep the wrap outside of the loop.

Now form the second half hitch by threading the working end into the second loop.

Then dress the knot before pulling both the half hitches to tighten.

Advantages

When you apply pressure to its standing part, this basic binding knot tends to hug the object you've tied it onto tightly. That fact makes it effective in situations where you do not want the knot moving from its original position when you tie it.

Disadvantages

In cases where you don't want a knot that constricts, such as when tying an animal, you cannot use this knot.

Possible applications

When hanging a hammock, you can use this knot to attach the ends of the ropes to two trees. Since this knot will constrict around the tree, the friction produced between the bark of the tree and the rope will prevent the rope from sliding down once you lie on the hammock.

If you are constructing a simple tarp shelter, you can use this knot to attach a rope's end to the tarp's grommet.

When camping, you can use the 2-half hitch to attach a tent's guy-lines to the rainfly.

#: Two-Half Hitch With A Bight

Being a handy variation to the two-half hitch described above, here's how to tie this knot:

How to tie

Hold the working end in your hand and then pass it around the object of your choice, like a pole or tree. The result will be a single turn.

Now proceed to pass the working end of the rope in front of its standing part.

Then thread the working end into the loop you created. Pull it to tighten.

Use the remaining part of your working end to form a bight. This step makes it easy to untie the knot. Pass it around the standing part, but ensure you keep the war outside the loop.

Then form the second half of the hitch by threading the bight through the loop you created.

Dress your knot, then pull both the half hitches to tighten.

Advantages

Although this knot is almost similar to the 2-half hitch, it is both easy and quick to untie and tie.

Disadvantages

Because this knot is easy to tie and untie, it could become loose, even in situations when you don't want it to be so. That, therefore, means it is less secure than the 2-half hitch.

Possible applications

You can use this knot for similar purposes as the 2 half-hitch knots. However, this specific variation can be useful in situations where you need to untie something quickly later. All you have to do is grab hold of the working end and pull it, which will, in turn, force the night to pull through the send ½ hitch, hence untying it.

#: The Round Turn And The 2-Half Hitch Knot

As another variation of the 2-half hitch knot, here's how to tie this knot:

How to tie

Start by passing your rope around an object to form a complete round turn as shown below

Now pass the working end of the rope in front of its standing part—shown below.

Then thread the working end into the loop formed in the previous step. Pull to tighten, which will form the first half of the hitch.

Now pass your working end around the standing part of the rope again, but this time, keep the wrap outside the loop.

Now thread the working end into the second loop you created above to form the second half hitch.

Dress the knot, then proceed to pull on the two half-hitches to tighten. Your knot is now complete and should look like the one shown below

Advantages

This variation offers more friction on the object onto which you've tied it. It, therefore, drastically reduces slipping by spreading the load's weight on the rope on two turns as opposed to one, which makes the knot stronger, thus less likely to break.

Disadvantages

Tying this knot takes longer than the two-half hitch, but the added strength makes up for this time.

Possible applications

You can use this knot in situations where you need to secure a rope to stationary objects. You can also use it in most situations where you use the two-half hitch, but with the added advantage of more surface area on an object, thus making the knot much stronger

As an example, you can use this knot to tie a boat to a cleat.

Chapter 5: Knots For Rock Climbers & Mountaineers

Below are knots ideal for mountaineers and rock climbers:

#: Figure 8 Follow-Through Knot

This knot is a variation of the figure 8 loop knot, but a bit more complex and secure.

How to tie

Start by tying a figure 8 knot on the working end of your rope. Ensure you leave at least a few inches of extra rope so that you can complete the 'follow-through' section of the knot. As you continue to practice, you will start getting a sense of how much rope you need to leave.

Pass your working end around—and through—the item you'd like the loop to encompass——shown below.

Loosen the figure 8 knot you made in step 1 to enlarge it slightly, an important step that will help you finish the remaining steps easily.

Now thread the working end through the spaces you created when you enlarged your figure-eight knot. The aim here is to retrace it, which means you should be precise as you do this. The image below shows you how your knot should look like after this step.

Now dress the knot by flipping the top strand of the rope near the standing part downwards. Your knot should look symmetrical when you look at it from both sides of the knot and both ends of the '8.'

Pull the knot to tighten it. Your knot is now complete

Optional steps

As an added measure of security and safety, you can tie a backup knot to the standing part of your rope using the extra portion of the working end.

How to tie

Hold both the working end and the standing part above the knot. Now cross your working end over the standing part—shown below.

Wrap the working end around and behind to the front. That will result in a wrap around your standing part. You will have formed a crossing point now.

Keep the crossing point between the figure 8 and the crossing point as shown below.

Now thread your working end through the two wraps. Ensure to pass it below the crossing points and away from the figure 8 knot—shown below.

Then pull on the working end of your rope to tighten and backup the knot. If you tie it correctly, it should look like an '=' on one side and an 'X' on the other side.

NOTE: This knot is intricate and used in very critical applications. After you tie it, you should inspect the knot thoroughly to ensure that you tied it correctly. You can even have someone double-check it for you.

Advantages

You can rely on this knot for more critical applications and when you want a more robust knot.

Disadvantages

This knot takes more time to tie than simpler knots such as the bowline. Additionally, you should take special attention to ensure you tie and dress this knot, especially if you are going to use it in critical applications.

Possible applications

This knot can be ideal in rock climbing and mountaineering based on how secure it is. However, you should get training from a qualified instructor before using it. You should also practice a lot before you apply it in a real-life situation.

There are many variations to the bowline knot. The one-handed bowline knot can come in handy in a case where you need to tie a bowline around the waist. To tie this knot, you should only use one hand—preferably your prominent hand.

How to tie

Start by holding the working end of your rope and passing it around your waist. Pass it in a way that ensures the working end is on the right side of your body, and the standing part of the rope is on the left side of your body.

Now ensure you hold the working end with your right hand. Leave about 7-8 inches of rope between the position you are holding and the end of the rope.

Cross the working end—still in your right hand—over the standing part of the rope on the left side of your body

With a twisting motion, bend your right wrist and move the working end over the standing part, then towards your belly button—shown below.

Using your thumb, hook the standing part of the rope.

Now slightly twist the rope in your right hand until you eventually end up with an overhand loop wrapped around your hand—shown below. The working end should be on the right side of the standing part.

Using your index finger, pass the working end of the rope behind the standing part.

Hook the working end using your thumb and bring it around the standing part.

Grab the working end and pull it to go through the loop that is now encircling your hand.

Now pull the knot as tightly as possible to complete your one-handed bowline.

Possible applications

Besides rock climbing and mountaineering, you can also use this knot in many other situations where you can only use one hand to make a knot.

You need to practice creating this knot until it becomes as easy as tying your shoelaces because, during an emergency, you will have to be very fast, and you will have to rely on your instincts and memory to tie the knot.

#: One-Handed Bowline For Fishing

Picture this:

You've gone fishing, and your boat/canoe capsizes., but you manage to hold onto something. Someone throws you a rope to rescue you, but you need to keep holding onto the object as you tie the rope around your waist.

In such a case, if you know how to tie the one-handed bowline, you can tie the rope around your waist quickly with one hand so that the person can pull you to the shore and safety.

#: Autoblock Knot

The autoblock knot is an easy-and-quick to tie friction knot mostly used as a backup for grapples. This knot is usually made using either temporary or factory-made loops to griping any direction and can be slid freely over a rope during a time of controlled descent.

How to tie

Wrap your autoblock cord around four to five times around your rappel ropes. Ensure you use a thin cord to do this—like the 5mm or the 6mm static cordage. Use most of the length of the cord on wrapping because the more wraps you make, the more friction generated.

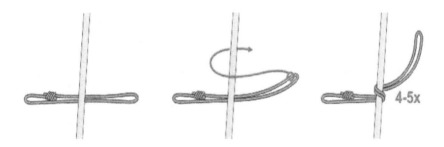

Clip both ends of your cord into your harness leg loop's locking carabiner. Lock the carabiner so that your cord doesn't become undone. Lastly, you should arrange all the wraps until they look neat – not crossing each other.

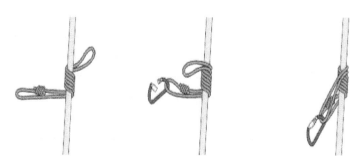

#: Valdotain Tresse knot

Also called the VT knot, the use of this friction knot is common when descending and ascending on ropes. It is most popular with arborists.

How to tie

Make at least 4 wraps around the main rope using a sewn prusik, spliced eye split tail, or hand-tied friction cord as shown in the image below

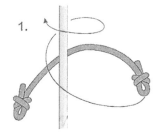

After doing the fourth wrap, bring the two ends down on the same level

Now cross the two lines in front of the main rope then cross them again at the back. That will add up to a total of 6 wraps

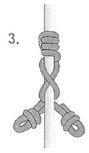

Join the eyes of your rope in front of the main rope and clip them together using a carabiner

#: Munter Hitch

This knot provides a method for rappelling and belaying without using a rappel/belay device. This knot works best with a large and pear-shaped carabiner, and you should only use it with a locking carabiner.

When belaying using this knot, you should ensure that the rope you are using to carry the load is next to the carabiner's spine. It is vital to set up this knot correctly before use because if set incorrectly, it may be life-threatening to the person at the end of this rope.

How to tie

Make a loop on your rope, then slip it into a locking carabiner. Create another loop with the part of the rope crossing opposite the loop you made first.

Now Slip the second loop you made into your carabiner and lock it

Ensure the strand of rope that carries the load is next to the spine of your carabiner—the strand with the red arrow below. Never put a load of the strand near the mechanism.

#: Klemheist Knot

To tie this knot, you first form a prusik loop—also discussed later in the book— with a rope or line that does not exceed half the diameter of the main rope. The result is a friction knot loop that can slide down the main rope without holding the knot (when no load is applied)

How to tie

Place the prusik loop behind your static rope/line.

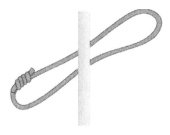

Now wrap the static line once using the loop, towards the right side—as shown below.

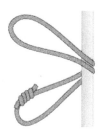

Now make two more loops around the main rope as you work your way from the bottom to the top.

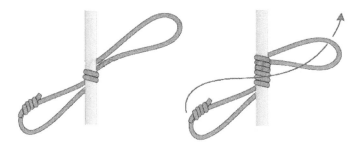

Feed the loop on the left side through the loop on the right side.

Pull the loop on the left side back over to the left of your main rope/line, then pull it down hard to set it, which should complete the knot.

Grasp the entire knot and slide it up on your mainline. Load and grip it to the mainline and add weight to the loop.

Chapter 6: Knots For Farms & Animals

The following knots are ideal for farm animals and farming-related applications:

#: Prusik Knot

Also called the prusik hitch, this knot can come in handy in situations where you want to attach an object on the standing part of a given length of rope. For this knot to work effectively, you should use a thinner rope than the main rope used.

How to tie

Start by deciding the size you want your loop to be, which will mostly depend on the number of times you'd like to wrap your loop around the main rope. The more wraps you will need, the larger the loop you will have to create.

Now cut a length of rope, leaving a few extra inches longer than the overall circumference you would like your loop to have.

Tie the ends of the rope you cut using the double fisherman's knot, as illustrated in the image below;

Then lay the loop you created above behind the main rope as shown below

Move the end of the loop that has the fisherman's knot around and over the main rope. The knot should pass through the loop, which results in a complete wrap around the main rope as shown in the image below

Repeat threading the end of the loop—as illustrated in the step above—for at least three more times. However, be very

careful as you do this, and ensure that every wrap you make does not cross over the previous one.

Having created the wraps around the main rope, double-check to see if they are lying neatly and not crossing over each other.

If they are okay, you can now proceed to apply tension to the end of the loop with the fisherman's knot. If some wraps do not look like they are snuggling up around the main rope tightly, you should try and manipulate them with your fingers.

NOTE: If you have tied this knot correctly, and you apply enough tension to the rope, then you should not be able to move the position of the knot along the main rope.

Advantages

You can easily attach this knot to a rope that already has tension applied to it. It is also useful because when you apply tension or a load to it, the friction produced hinders it from sliding on the main rope.

Another advantage is that when you remove tension, the knot can easily slide to another position along the main rope.

Disadvantages

If you do not apply enough tension on the knot, the knot can unintentionally move from the position you originally tied it to on the main rope.

Another disadvantage is that if you use a rope that is either icy or wet, the knot may be susceptible to slipping since this knot depends on the friction generated between the main rope and the secondary rope. The type of rope you use can also make the knot either less or more effective since different ropes have different friction-generating abilities.

Possible applications

In farms, you can use it to secure mules or horses to a Highline rope. You can achieve this by attaching a tight line between 2 trees. You should then proceed to attach the prusik knots at different intervals along the line. That will make it easier to space out each of your animals evenly—based on the fact that the knot is easy to reposition; it also holds its own when animals try to pull on it.

You can also use this knot in rock climbing and mountaineering. If you choose to use it for this purpose, you should get a qualified instructor to train you on how to use it safely.

When making a shelter that has a tarp draped over the rigid line, you can use a prusik knot on both ends of the rigid line to help you keep your tarp stretched tight.

#: The Miller's Loop

The miller loop is another important farm knot used to close up half-empty bags of feed or grain by bunching the top of the bag into a neck and fastening it.

How to tie

Wrap your rope around the neck of the bag. Create a crossing point with the working end and the standing part—shown below.

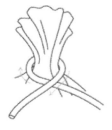

Circle the neck of the bag once more with the working end of your rope. Now slip the working end under the coils (loosen them if necessary).

Now pull the two ends of the rope to tighten your knot

#: Halter Hitch

This knot can tether an animal to a rail using a rope attached to a halter.

How to tie

Drape the working end of your rope over the rail, then pass the working end over the standing part. That will form the main loop of your knot.

Now pass the working end behind the main loop to create a second loop.

Then form a bight with the rope near your working end and pass it over the main loop then into the second loop.

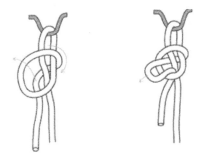

Now pull on the standing end and the bight to tighten your knot. The knot is now complete.

To untie this knot, you just have to pull the running end, which, although convenient for farmers, can be a problem with intelligent animals. You can secure the knot by inserting the working end into the bight.

#: Farmer's Loop

You can use this knot to make a knot in the middle part of a rope. You can use it as a handhold or even as a place to attach your tools as well as other objects.

That's not all, you can also tie this knot on a rope to take up the slack or to isolate weak sections of a rope.

The main advantage of using this knot is that it is easy to tie and untie.

How to tie

Start by wrapping your rope around the palm of your hand three times. Leave the working end of the rope hanging from your hand.

Lift the loop in the middle to overlap the loop on the right. The right loop now becomes the middle loop.

Likewise, pull the loop that is now in the middle to overlap the left loop.

Repeat by pulling the middle loop to overlap the right one.

Finally, pull the middle loop to overlap the left loop. Pull the loop out a little further to make it to your desired size.

Slide the knot gently out of your hand, then pull on the loop and the ends to tighten the knot

#: The Poacher's Knot

Also called the strangle snare or the poacher's snare, if you find yourself in a situation where you need to catch small animals for survival, then this knot might come in handy. It creates a noose that you can use to snare small animals.

How to tie

Pass your working end over to the standing part of your rope to create a loop—shown below.

Now pinch the crossing point with your index finger and thumb.

Form a wrap using the working end around the loop—shown below. The point at which the working end crosses over itself creates an X.

Now create another partial wrap using your working end around the loop—shown below. Keep the wrap in the direction of the loop and not toward the standing end.

Next, stop pinching the rope. Pass the working end through the two wraps. Ensure that the working end passes below the X you created earlier.

Now pull on the working end gently, ensuring that you do not tighten your knot all the way. Your knot is now complete. If you tied the knot correctly, it should be able to slide easily on the standing part. If it feels hard, then you've probably tightened it too much.

Advantages

This knot is easy to tie, and the loop it creates lock tightly when pulled. That means if you use it to trap an animal, the harder it pulls, the tighter the loop gets.

Disadvantages

The knot's design makes it a good, tight fit. However, once it tightens, it may be tough to loosen the noose; hence, you might have to cut the cordage.

Possible applications

As mentioned earlier, you can use this knot to catch small animals using snares. If you are going to use it for this purpose, you must avoid tightening the knot too much. By leaving this knot loose, it will be able to slide along the standing part smoothly and quickly, which will allow it to constrict easily around the animals that run through your snare.

As an added advantage, when the animal struggles, trying to free itself when it feels the noose tighten, the knot will tighten further, making it difficult or even impossible for the animal to escape.

You can use this knot as a binding knot if you make a variation to the procedure by tightening the knot around the standing part. You can use it in situations such as tying two lengths of paracord, and then after rolling up your sleeping pad or bag, you can place the loop of each of the ropes around your bedding.

As you pull on the standing end, the knot will constrict, thus keeping your bedding rolled up neatly. When you need to unroll it, you just have to pinch the knot and pull it firmly to slide it up.

Chapter 7: Knots For Shoes

NOTE: In this chapter, we refer to the yellow lace o as the left lace and the blue lace as the right shoelace—from the perspective of the person wearing the shoe.

#: The Starting Knot

Almost all shoelace knots use the left-over-right starting knot, also called the 'overhand knot' or 'a half knot.' This knot is the base for all knots discussed in this chapter:

How to tie

Hold one lace in your right hand and the other in your left hand. Cross the working end of the left lace over the working end of the right shoelace to form a crossing point.

Wrap the tight working end around the front of the left working end, which will end up at the back of the gap formed between the two laces.

Pass the right lace through the gap between the two laces until it gets to the front right-hand side.

Now pull both ends to complete and tighten the knot.

#: The Standard Shoelace Knot

Also referred to as the loop, swoop and pull or the Bunny Rabbit knot, this is one of the most used knots to tie shoes.

How to tie

Begin with a starting knot—explained earlier.

Now form the right working end into a bight—as shown below.

Pass the left working end behind the right loop.

Create a wrap around the right loop with the left lace so that it ends up in front.

Now push the left lace into the hole formed between the two laces—as shown below.

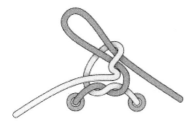

Pull the left lace from the side until it comes out to form another loop. Now you have two loose loops.

Then grab both the right and left loop and pull them to tighten and complete the knot

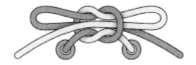

#: Double Shoelace Knot

The double shoelace knot also called the shoe clerk's knot, is a crude way of making a knot consume excess lace to prevent the ends from dragging, which makes it quite bulky

How to tie

Begin by making the standard shoelace knot as described earlier. Make your loops long enough to work with, in the next steps.

.

Now cross the left loop over the front of your right loop as shown below

Wrap the right loop around the back of the left loop then feed its end into the gap between the two laces

You have just formed another overhand knot on top of the first one. Pull the two ends of the loops to tighten your knot.

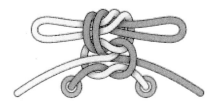

#: Boat Shoe Knot

Also called the heaving line knot, Eastland knot, or the barrel tassel, use of this knot is common on deck shoes—boat shoes—or on moccasins that have leather laces. Instead of the usual knots, it creates decorative coils. It works by coiling each end of the lace around itself until there's no more lace.

How to tie

Unlike all the other shoe-related knots, this knot does not start with the starting knot.

On the contrary, you start by forming one end of your lace into a loop by doubling it back onto itself. However, you should ensure that you leave a long enough working end. You will have a better idea of the length to leave as you continue practicing.

You should note that making this loop too long will make the working end too short and unable to finish completing all the wraps required to cover the loop. On the other hand, if the loop is too short, you won't have enough room to spend the excess lace. You will end up with a tiny coil and a long working end protruding from the top of your knot.

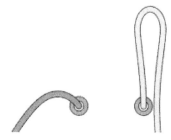

Wrap the end of your shoelace once around the lower part of the loop you formed. In this case, the direction of the wrap does not matter. You can wrap it either way—around the back or the front.

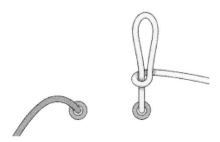

Wrap the end of the shoelace again around the loop immediately above the first one you made

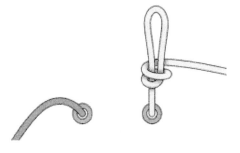

Continue to wind the end of your lace around the loop until it gets to the top. As you do this, ensure you make it as tight as possible around the loop and as snuggly as possible against previous loops, which will result in a tight coil of lace.

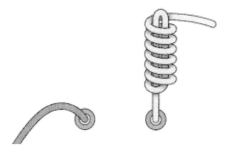

Feed the end of your shoelace through the remaining top of your loop. You can now pull the whole coil upwards. That will pinch the top of your loop tightly to secure the loose end.

Repeat all the above steps with the other lace to end up with two separate coils—as shown below.

NOTE: To make this knot more secure, you should wrap your coils starting from the furthest bottom of your loops (touching the shoe eyelet). However, doing this will affect the overall appearance of your knots as they will end up sticking out from your shoe like antennae instead of loosely dangling as shown in the last image above.

https://www.fieggen.com/shoelace/boatshoeknot.htm

#: Better Bow Knot

The better bow knot is a secure shoelace knot based on looping around more than one time.

How to tie

Begin with the starting knot.

Now form a loop using the working end of the right lace by doubling it back onto itself as shown below.

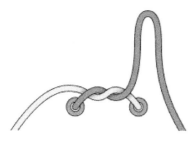

Pass the left lace around and behind the right one.

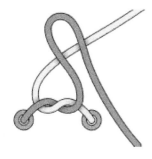

Use the left lace to make a turn around the right loop so that it ends up in front. Up to this part, this knot follows the same procedure as the standard shoelace knot—the main difference shows in the next step.

Unlike in the standard shoelace knot where you only make 1 turn around the loop, in this case, you will have to pass the left lace around the right loop once more.

Pass the left lace around the right loop so that it ends up Infront again.

Now feed the left lace into the loop it formed as shown below.

Continue to feed the left lace through the space you created until its loop emerges on the right side of the knot

Pull the two loops to tighten your knot to end up with a knot that is neat as the one shown below.

NOTE: The finished knot should be very tight and closed. It should have a double wrap in the middle—in contrast to the single knot on other simpler shoelace knots.

Chapter 8: Necktie Knots

Knots for neckties have significant variations in size, shape, and symmetry for different knots.

Therefore, when making a necktie knot, you should consider the length of the tie, the thickness of the material used to make the tie, and the desired look. Every knot has a distinct character. Thick ties will usually require you to use smaller knots while thinner ties will look better with larger knots.

Below are some of the most common knots you can use to tie your tie:

#: The Four In Hand Knot

The four in hand knot is the most common necktie knot that people use because it is simple to tie and can be ideal for most of the occasions. The knot is slender and slightly asymmetrical. The name of the knot comes from the name of a gentleman's club founded in the 19th century.

How to tie

Begin with the small end of your tie on your left and the wide end on your right. Make the small end lie somewhat above your belly button, which may vary depending on your height and the thickness and length of your tie. Note that you will only be moving the working end of the tie (the wide end).

Now pass the working end over the small end -towards the left.

Pass the working end under the small end—towards the right.

Continue moving the working end across the front and towards the left.

From underneath the neck loop, move the working end upwards.

Move it back down into the loop you made now formed in the front (loosen a little bit if necessary)

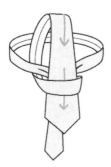

Now pull the working end downwards to tighten the knot. Slide the knot upwards to adjust.

#: The Eldredge Knot

This knot is eye-catching, complex, and unorthodox. Invented in 2007 by Jeffrey Eldredge, it became famous on the internet in 2008. As opposed to most of the necktie knots, the Eldredge knot uses the small end of the tie as the working end. When completed, you tuck the excess small end away behind the shirt collar.

Regarding size, this knot is large and creates a tapered fishtail braid effect. You should wear this tie with a lot of caution as it does not suit some occasions.

How to tie

Begin with the small end of the tie on the right and the wide end on you the left. Adjust the tie so that the tip of the wide end rests at the top of your belt buckle. In this section, the working end will be the small end of your tie.

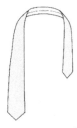

Now pass the small end over to the wide end —towards the left.

Pass the small end under the wide end —towards the right.

Continue moving it towards the neck loop up to the center.

Move it into the neck loop then towards the left.

Pass it across the front, then to the right. From underneath, Move it upwards into the neck loop.

Move it downwards to the left, then around the back of the wide end, towards the right; do not tighten this part.

Pass the small end across the front, then to the left, and finally, through the loop you created in the previous step.

Pull the small end of the tie to the left to tighten.

Continue to pass it up to the center, then towards and into the neck loop, and then finally pass it to the left.

Move it upwards to the center, towards the neck loop. Pass it downwards through the neck loop and towards the right. Do not tighten this part.

Pass it across the front of the tie to the left then through the loop you created in the step above.

Pull the working end to the left to tighten your knot.

Tuck the excess part of the small end behind the left side of the neck loop.

#: Van Wijk Knot

This necktie knot is cylindrical and incredibly tall. Its invention came by because of an attempt to come up with the tallest wearable tie knot possible by an artist called Lisa Van Wijk. When tied correctly, this knot creates an unmistakable and striking helical effect.

How to tie

Begin by placing the small end of your tie on the left and the wide end on the right. Adjust the tie such that the tip of the small end is resting slightly above your belly button. That, however, may vary depending on your height and the thickness and length of your tie. The working end is the wide end of your tie.

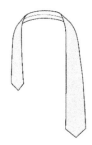

Pass the wide end over the small end – towards the left.

Continue to pass it under the small end, then towards the right.

Pass it across the front of the tie then towards the left.

Pass it under the small end, then move it towards the right.

Pass it across the front of the tie then towards the left.

Pass it under the small end, then towards the right.

Pass it across the front of the tie again, then towards the left.

From underneath, move it upwards through the neck loop.

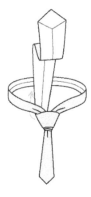

Pass it downward then under the three loops now formed in front of the tie (loosen if necessary).

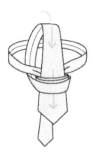

Pull down on the wide end of the tie to tighten the knot. Slide your knot upwards to adjust. It is normal for the first and second loop on the knot to show slightly under the third loop.

#: **The Trinity Knot**

Just like the Eldredge knot, the trinity knot is a recent innovation also tied using the small end as the working end and tied very loosely initially then pulled to tighten at the end.

This knot produces a slightly asymmetrical and rounded shape. It is visually striking and slightly larger than some common necktie knots.

How to tie

Begin by placing the small end of your tie to the right and the wide end to the left. Adjust the tie so that the tip of the wide end rests at the top of your belt buckle. For these instructions, you will only be using the small end.

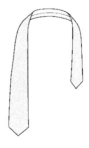

Pass the small end over the wide end, then towards the left.

From underneath, Pass it upwards into the neck loop.

Pass it downwards and towards the left.

Pass it around the back of your wide end, then towards the right.

Move it upwards to the center then into the neck loop.

Pass it through the neck loop then downwards towards the left.

Pass it across the front of the wide end then upwards into the neck loop.

Pass it downwards through the loop you formed above. Do not tighten it.

Pass the small end behind the wide end —towards the right.

Bring it across the front of the wide end towards the center.
Pass it through the loop you created in the step above.

Tighten your knot and tuck the excess part of the small end behind the left side of your neck loop

#: Bow Tie Knot

The use of bow ties become more popular at the end of the 19th century. Back then, people wore white bowties with evening tails and black bowties with dinner jackets.

Today, bowties are common during formal occasions, but its popularity for everyday wear has also been rising. A bowtie is perfect for you if you like to stand out among your peers.

How to tie

Begin by placing the bowtie lying face up. Adjust it such that the right side is slightly shorter than the left side. Here, we shall refer to the end on the right as B and the end on the left as A.

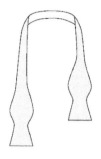

Move side A on top of B to the right.

Pass A under B then upwards through the neck loop.

At the joint, fold side B to the right then towards the left to create a bow shape.

Bring side A downwards and over the middle of the bow
shape created using side B.

Fold side A backward to your chest and pinch at the fold.

Push the end of side A (that you are pinching) into the loop
now behind side B.

To tighten, pull on the folded parts of the bow.

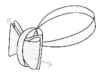

Adjust until you balance both sides of the bow.

Conclusion

Thank you for reading this guide.